Robertaoconnell7@gmail.com

Illustrations and Story by: Roberta M. O'Connell

Aka: Auntie Roberta

Printed in the USA *=

Thank you for purchasing this book.

May you be Blessed with Peace, Joy and Much Love,

Auntie Roberta

Aa

A is for April,
that's me !

Bb

B is for
butterfly,
flying free.

3

Cc

C c is for crayon,
I use to color.

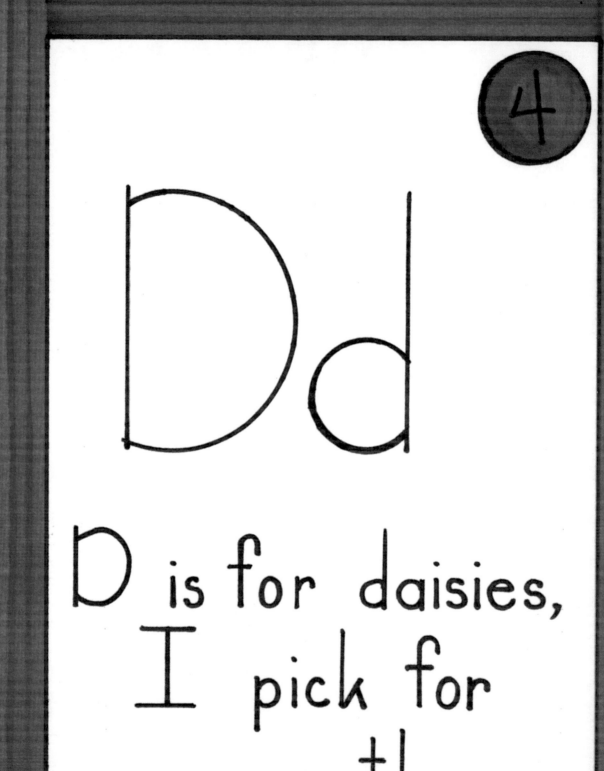

4

Dd

D is for daisies,
I pick for
my mother.

E e

E is for elf,
in Santa's workshop.

Ff

F is for
fun, like
when I hop.

G g

G is for goat,
whose name is Billy.

Hh

H is for hat,
that looks real silly!

I i

I is for ink,
that's in my pen.

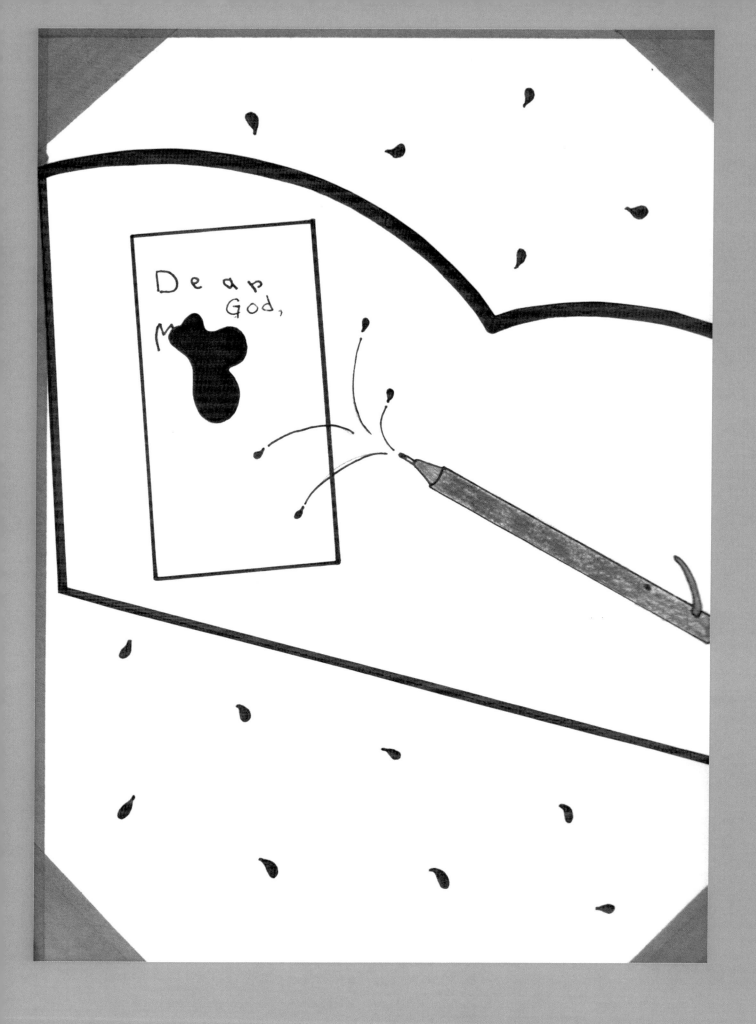

J j

J is for joke,

I want to

hear again!

K k

K is for King, with a golden crown.

L l

L is for love,
that   we
should spread around.

Mm

M is for music,
I like to play.

Nn

N is for notes,
that show me
the way.

O is for owl, who

is very wise.

P p

P is for present,
I get as a
surprise!

Qq

Q is for quilt,
upon my bed.

18

R r

R is for rainbow,
of blue, green & red.

S s

S is for swan,
with beautiful wings.

T t

T is for teacher,
who teaches
me things.

21

U u

U is for
umbrella,
that keeps me dry.

V is for vest, Daddy wears with a tie.

Ww

W is for wiggle,
when I wiggle
my toes.

X x

X is for x-ray, that shows you your bones.

Yy

Y is for yo-yo, that goes up and down.

Z z

Z is for zebra,
with stripes all around.

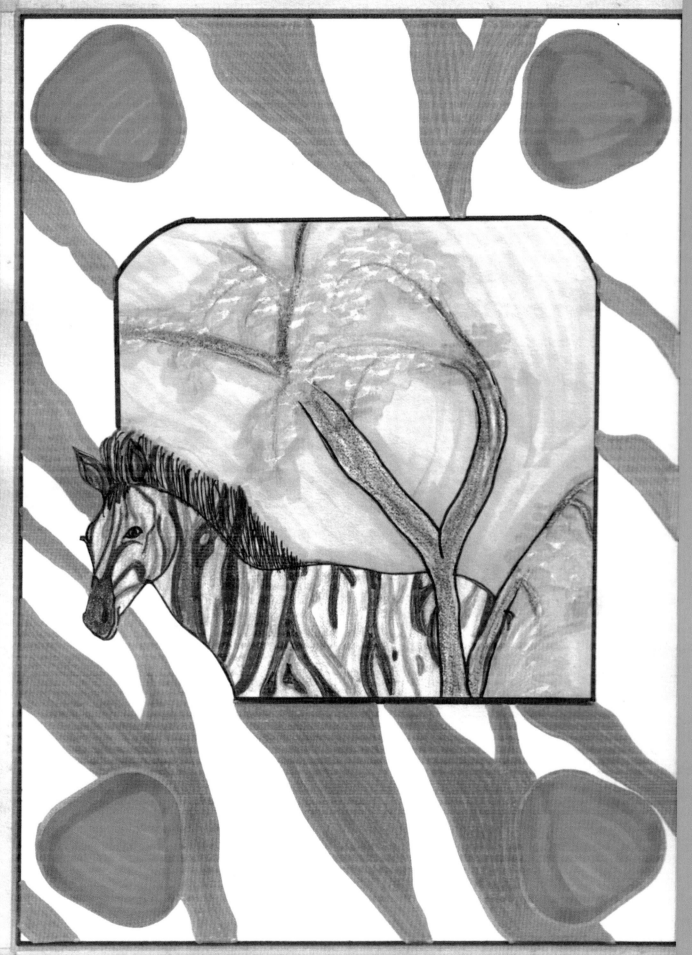

My Kitties: (top) HOBO, (bottom) PEANUT

Made in United States
North Haven, CT
29 November 2024

61178910R00031